Women Starting Business 2024

COPYRIGHT

All rights reserved. No part of this publication may be reproduced, distributed, or transmitted in any form or by any means, including photocopying, recording, or other electronic or mechanical methods, without the prior written permission of the publisher, except in the case of brief quotations embodied in critical review and certain other noncommercial uses permitted by copyright law.

Copyright © Sharon Glynn, 2024

DISCLAIMER

This book offers information for your general knowledge and is not a substitute for professional advice. Sharon Glynn worked hard to provide accurate and complete content, but we can't guarantee that it's perfect or fits every situation. So, if you're thinking about making any big moves or trying out the strategies we talk about, it's a good idea to chat with experts like financial or legal advisors first.

Also, this book is filled with stories and insights from my own life, but remember, what worked for me might not work exactly the same for you. Feel free to tweak the ideas here to better fit your own situation and ambitions.

WOMEN STARTING BUSINESS 2024

The Female Beginners Guide To A Successful Entrepreneur

&

BONUS

By Sharon Glynn

Women Starting Business 2024

BONUS

Here's a list of 20 fresh entrepreneurial concepts for women in 2024, spanning different sectors and keeping up with the latest trends:

Green Wardrobe Shop: Handpick and retail fashion that's both sustainable and ethically produced, including clothes, accessories, and beauty items.

Holistic Online Coaching: Offer virtual guidance in wellness, focusing on diet, exercise, and mental health through online sessions and tailored plans.

Digital Gala Organizer: Specialize in orchestrating online gatherings such as seminars, nuptials, and business events, using cutting-edge digital tools.

Telecommuting Consultancy: Advise companies on enhancing their remote work setups and offer tech solutions for better productivity and teamwork.

Earth-Friendly Household Items: Market home essentials that are kind to the planet, like biodegradable kitchen tools, non-toxic cleaners, and waste-reducing products.

Web-Based Marketing Firm: Launch a service focused on online marketing, helping small enterprises with social media, content creation, search engine optimization, and web ads.

Virtual Learning Hub: Create a digital space for learning with classes, seminars, and materials on entrepreneurship, self-improvement, and artistic abilities.

Curated Subscription Boxes: Assemble and distribute themed boxes on a subscription basis, filled with unique items like fine snacks, handmade goods, or green living must-haves.

Online Support Services: Offer remote assistance for businesses and professionals, handling tasks like correspondence, scheduling, and project management.

Pet Care Ventures: Provide services for pet owners such as pet-sitting, walks, grooming, and training, or sell organic pet products online.

Home Styling Advice: Offer online home decor advice, creating design plans and helping clients revamp their living or workspaces.

Wellness and Exercise Apps: Build an app that delivers custom fitness routines, diet monitoring, relaxation practices, and a supportive user community.

Web-Based Mental Health Support: Offer virtual therapy sessions for those looking for help with mental wellness, stress relief, and personal growth.

Gourmet Homemade Goods: Start crafting and selling your own line of gourmet treats like fine chocolates, homemade preserves, exotic teas, or gluten-free pastries.

Immersive Virtual Content: Create virtual reality content for entertainment, education, travel, or training, tapping into the growing market for VR experiences.

Senior Support Services: Set up an agency that provides personalized care for the elderly, helping them with daily tasks and offering companionship.

Online Study Assistance: Support students with online tutoring, homework aid, and additional educational resources to complement remote learning.

Natural Cosmetics Line: Develop a beauty brand with natural and organic products, emphasizing clean ingredients and ethical production.

Digital Media Production: Start an agency that produces digital content, including videos, photos, graphics, and social media collateral for clients.

ABOUT THE AUTHOR

Meet Sharon Glynn, far more than just a name. She's a trailblazer, a partner in life, and a nurturing parent. Sharon's path, paved with grit, creativity, and an unwavering quest for economic independence, shines as a source of motivation for women across the globe. Sharon stands tall as a pioneer in the business realm, breaking barriers and lifting the ceiling for ambitious women everywhere. Her ventures haven't just reshaped markets; they've ignited a fearless drive in countless women to chase their dreams. With an instinct for spotting potential and a fire for innovation, Sharon has forged her own way to triumph, making an everlasting impression on the world of business. But it's not all work for Sharon. She cherishes her time as a spouse and mom, masterfully juggling the thrills of family life with the hustle of a business mogul. She's a living example of how to blend aspiration with heart, resolve with kindness. What drives Sharon is a deep-seated passion to boost women's empowerment. She's more than a billionaire; she's a forward-thinking giver who's set on sparking societal progress. Convinced that financial liberation can revolutionize lives, Sharon is on a mission to ensure every woman can tap into her potential and carve out her own success story. Sharon Glynn is the embodiment of strength, tenacity, and warmth. Her narrative is a powerful reminder of the immense possibilities within us all, urging women to seize their power, follow their bliss, and craft the existence they dream of. Come along with Sharon Glynn as she leads the charge for women's empowerment, one entrepreneurial venture at a time.

Table of Contents

INTRODUCTION **13**
MONEY MINDSET **19**
THINKING LIKE AN ENTREPRENEUR **29**
YOUR BRAIN AND BUSINESS **33**
BECOMING YOUR OWN FUTURE **37**
YOUR VALUE PROPOSITION **43**
TRANSFER OF WEALTH **49**
CAREGIVING AND LONGEVITY **55**
HOW TO BE PAID WHAT YOU ARE WORTH **61**
WRITING YOUR BUSINESS PLAN **67**
BECOMING AUTHENTIC **77**
PHILANTHROPY **83**
RETIREMENT **87**

INTRODUCTION

Welcome aboard "Women Starting Business 2024," an in-depth journey into the vibrant world of starting businesses, viewed through the prism of female empowerment and cutting-edge innovation. In this collection of discussions, we'll be unpacking the shifting roles of women in the realm of commerce, spotlighting both the hurdles and breakthroughs, as well as the groundbreaking tactics that are charting new courses for their business ventures in 2024 and the years that follow.

As we set sail on this voyage, we're extending an open invitation for you to celebrate the tenacity, inventiveness, and drive of women business owners across the globe. From trailblazing new ventures to well-established firms, these women are at the forefront of innovation, making significant marks on their sectors, and redefining the usual business molds.

Our "Female Entrepreneurs Forge Ahead 2024" initiative is all about kindling the entrepreneurial spirit within women, encouraging them to embrace their business dreams with boldness and resolve.

With a mix of thought-provoking dialogues, tales of triumph, and actionable guidance, we're diving into the ways female business leaders are navigating challenges, capitalizing on prospects, and influencing the commerce landscape amidst ongoing global shifts.

This series is crafted for anyone with a stake in entrepreneurship or a supporter of gender parity, aiming to educate, motivate, and stir up enthusiasm for the cause of female entrepreneurship. Let's honor the influential role of women launching businesses in 2024 and look forward to what lies ahead.

HISTORY OF FEMALE ENTREPRENEUR

Women who start and run their own companies are known as female entrepreneurs. Over the years, especially throughout the 20th and into the

21st century, there's been a noticeable uptick in the number of businesses owned by women in the U.S. Since 1997, we've seen these businesses popping up at a growth rate of about 5% each year. This surge has paved the way for a number of successful self-made women, including the likes of fashion icon Coco Chanel, business mogul Diane Hendricks, tech leader Meg Whitman, and media powerhouse Oprah Winfrey.

Eliza Lucas Pinckney was a trailblazer back in 1739 when, at just 16, she took the reins of her family's plantations in South Carolina, marking the first known instance of a woman-owned business in the US. Throughout the 18th and 19th centuries, women often ran small enterprises out of necessity, either to supplement their income or to fend off poverty, especially after losing a spouse.

These early female business ventures, however, weren't really seen as entrepreneurial. Many women, particularly Black women facing significant societal and educational barriers, especially in the segregation-era South, carved out entrepreneurial roles for themselves in fields like dressmaking, hair care, and midwifery.

The term "entrepreneur" initially applied exclusively to men, but over time, women began to break into the business world. This shift was gradual and reflected a changing societal acceptance of women in business roles. For example, in the 17th century, Dutch women in what's now New York City inherited wealth and became business owners. Margaret Hardenbrook Philipse was one of the most successful, engaging in trading and shipowning.

In the mid-1700s, women commonly owned businesses like brothels and taverns, though these were often stigmatized. Nevertheless, women like Rebecca Lukens, who took over a family steel business in 1825, defied societal expectations and thrived. By the 1900s, the rise of feminism helped normalize the idea of female entrepreneurs, leading to success stories like Madame C. J. Walker, who became the first African American woman millionaire through her hair care products.

World War II saw many women stepping into roles left vacant by men, with some, like fashion designer

Pauline Trigere and beauty mogul Estée Lauder, launching successful businesses. Post-war, women continued to make inroads into entrepreneurship, supported by organizations like the National Federation of Business and Professional Women's Clubs. Women like Lillian Vernon and Mary Crowley innovated by starting home-based businesses, while others, like Bette Nesmith of "Mistake Out" fame, cleverly navigated gender biases.

The latter part of the 20th century saw women like Mary Kay Ash and Ruth Fertel of Ruth's Chris Steak House stepping up as entrepreneurs during challenging times, such as the Great Depression and the rise in divorce rates.

By the 1980s and 1990s, the hard work of countless women began to pay off, with legislation like the Women's Business Ownership Act of 1988 breaking down barriers in lending and government contracting.

The advent of the internet in the 1990s gave women in business a significant boost, yet challenges remained. The 2008 economic downturn didn't help, but the ongoing support for female entrepreneurs through educational programs and organizations continues to offer resources and support.

Since 2000, there's been a noticeable uptick in both small and large ventures started by women, with financing remaining a significant hurdle. Entrepreneurs like Vartika Manasvi highlight the opportunities and challenges faced by women in business, with some choosing to launch their ventures in places like Canada for its perceived advantages.

MONEY MINDSET

In 2024, the attitude toward money among women business owners is pivotal, especially as they launch new ventures. Let's talk about how this money mindset plays out for female entrepreneurs:

Mindset Evolution: Women in business are increasingly aware of the need to adopt a positive and robust attitude toward finances. This means moving past old, restrictive thoughts about money and welcoming a sense of plenty, opportunity, and financial strength.

Breaking Through Old Beliefs: It's common for women to encounter deep-seated notions about money that stem from cultural norms, how they were raised, or previous experiences. These thoughts, like "money is hard to come by" or "handling finances isn't my strong suit," can be obstacles to success. In 2024, women are actively working to recognize and push past these barriers to develop a more optimistic and expansive view of money.

Affirming Self-Worth: Female entrepreneurs are getting better at acknowledging their own worth and right to financial prosperity. This means valuing their skills, knowledge, and contributions in the marketplace and trusting that they should be financially compensated for their hard work and results.

Money as a Means to an End: There's a trend in 2024 where money is seen not just as a success indicator or a safety net but as a catalyst for empowerment and change. Women in business are using money strategically to expand their companies, follow their dreams, and make a positive mark in their communities and beyond.

Prioritizing Financial Know-How: With a solid money mindset, women business owners are putting financial education at the forefront in 2024. They're actively learning about essential financial principles, managing their funds wisely, and making savvy choices about investing, saving, and budgeting to grow and enhance their ventures.

A New Definition of Success: The idea of success in business isn't just about the bottom line anymore. While financial gain is still a key aim, women entrepreneurs in 2024 are also seeking fulfillment, purpose, balance between work and life, and societal contribution. They're aligning their financial perspectives with a broader vision of success that includes overall happiness and contentment.

Creating Wealth for the Future: Female business owners see the chance to create wealth and leave a legacy through their endeavors in 2024. By fostering a healthy attitude toward money and making smart financial moves, they're setting the stage for enduring wealth, security, and opportunities for the coming generations.

Community and Mentorship: In 2024, women entrepreneurs are drawing strength and support from networks and mentorship initiatives that focus on the financial mindset. By connecting with peers and mentors who share similar values and objectives, they're exchanging ideas, providing mutual support, and encouraging a resilient and positive approach to finances.

In essence, in 2024, women entrepreneurs are tapping into the transformative power of a constructive financial mindset to tackle obstacles, grab hold of opportunities, and achieve lasting success in their business pursuits. By changing how they view and interact with money, they're equipping themselves to craft a future rich in abundance, influence, and satisfaction.

6 IMPORTANT MONEY MINDSET A WOMAN SHOULD HAVE

I've come to terms with my previous financial blunders: You see, we're all prone to trip up now and then – it's simply part of the human experience. The thrill of entrepreneurship partly lies in discovering what strategies succeed and which ones flop.

When you're just starting out, it's a shot in the dark to pinpoint exactly what your venture needs. And even with the best planning, life can throw curveballs, like an unforeseen global health crisis or a shipment of goods that's just not up to scratch.

No matter the nature of your business slip-ups, it's possible to push past them. Rather than wallowing in regret or self-reproach, allow yourself some grace and look at each error as an opportunity for growth, something that can propel your business even further.

I'm dedicated to overcoming my financial hang-ups: These hang-ups are those pesky, deep-seated beliefs about money that just don't do you any favors. Holding these beliefs doesn't make them accurate, though.

Take it from me – I once thought that the only way to earn more was to log in more hours, especially with a baby to care for. This mindset had me working 10–12 hour days, which left me exhausted and absent from my family life.

Eventually, I changed my tune, convincing myself that it was indeed possible to make more money in just five hours a day. This shift allowed me to collect my son from daycare and enjoy some precious 'me time.'

It wasn't an overnight transformation to tackle this belief, but I'm proud to say those marathon workdays are behind me.

The first step to tackling these financial hang-ups is to identify them. So grab a pen and paper or open a new document on your computer, and start scribbling down every thought that pops up. Work on turning these thoughts into something more constructive.

I have the right to delegate aspects of my business: This can be a tough pill to swallow, especially if you're flying solo or self-employed. Sometimes you think you can't afford to bring someone else on board, or you figure it's not worth it because the task doesn't take up much of your time.

But the truth is, outsourcing can free you to focus on the unique aspects of your business that only you can advance. It doesn't matter if you're good at these tasks or even enjoy them.

If the thought of outsourcing makes you nervous, start with something small or choose a job that would clearly benefit from a professional touch, like accounting. You could also opt for automated software to handle routine tasks – it's cost-effective for your business budget.

I won't feel bad about employing a nanny: This one goes out to all the moms who grapple with guilt when it comes to leaving their kids to work. I've been there – trying to balance a baby on my lap while typing away. But this isn't just about childcare.

Consider hiring someone to clean, cook, or handle your grocery deliveries. These services can free you up to focus on your business, or at least clear your mind for the tasks ahead.

I'm entitled to carve out business development time: Working on your business involves evaluating your current operations and considering changes to your systems or processes. Maybe your scheduling software isn't making the cut anymore, and it's time to upgrade to something that lets clients book consultations and pay you simultaneously.

Growth also means investing time in yourself and your enterprise. There's a wealth of courses out there to enhance your operations, and getting a coach to navigate through challenges can be incredibly beneficial. Begin by setting aside short intervals for these activities. Even if you're not sure what you're looking for, commit to this time regardless.

I'm fully equipped to manage a business that aligns with my life goals: Sure, running a business is fantastic, but let's not forget one of its key purposes – to support your life ambitions. Maybe you're aiming for a flexible schedule to pick up your kids from school, or perhaps you're saving to launch a nonprofit in your community.

Whatever your personal aspirations, it's perfectly fine to strive for them – allow your business to be the vehicle that gets you there. Navigating the financial mindset in business is no cakewalk. It demands commitment and regular reminders, but trust me, it's absolutely worth the effort.

THINKING LIKE AN ENTREPRENEUR

Fostering Inventiveness: We want to inspire female entrepreneurs to tap into their creative powers when tackling problems and brainstorming new concepts. It's crucial to stress the value of unconventional thinking and using their distinct viewpoints and life stories to bring fresh ideas to the table in their respective fields.

Transforming Obstacles into Stepping Stones: For women embarking on business ventures, it's a game-changer to reframe obstacles as chances to learn and innovate. We should underline the need for grit and flexibility when dealing with difficulties and how to convert them into milestones of success.

Boosting Self-Belief: It's about empowering female entrepreneurs to have faith in their visions and competencies. They need see their worth and know-how, nudging them to follow their gut and make bold moves to chase their business dreams.

Seeking Guidance and Solidarity: The need for mentorship and support from those who've been there and done that should be champion. It's key for women to forge robust networks and be surrounded by mentors ready to provide direction, wisdom, and a cheerleading squad on their entrepreneurial path.

Embracing Smart Risk-Taking: Women at the startup helm should get comfortable with smart risk-taking and stepping beyond their safety zones. They should be encouraged to smartly evaluate risks, consider possible results, and make well-thought-out strides to push their ventures ahead.

Adopting a Learner's Attitude: A learner mindset should be cultivated in female entrepreneurs, with a focus on the idea that skills and smarts can grow with hard work and persistence. They need to be encouraged to love learning, seek out constructive criticism, and keep honing both themselves and their businesses.

Jumping on Opportunities: Female entrepreneurs needs to be motivated to actively grab opportunities and ride the wave of market trends. They should keep an ear to the ground on industry shifts, spot needs that haven't been met, and be the first to offer solutions and plug those gaps.

Highlighting Steadfastness: It's essential to talk up the importance of staying steadfast in entrepreneurship, especially for women who might face unique hurdles. They should be encouraged to keep going when times get tough, learn from missteps, and keep a hopeful attitude as they stride toward their business aims.

Encouraging Teamwork: The perks of working together for female entrepreneurs should be pointed out. It's beneficial for them to look for teamwork chances with other companies, groups, and folks who can pool different strengths and resources for the win-win.

Creating Meaningful Change: Female entrepreneurs should be inspired to line up their business goals with a grander purpose and vision for societal, environmental, and economic betterment. They should think about how their business can be a force for good, championing sustainability and uplifting their communities.

YOUR BRAIN AND BUSINESS

"Your Brain And Business under Women Starting Business" delves into the intriguing nexus of brain science and business creation, specifically curated for women taking the entrepreneurial plunge. We'll dive into how a deep grasp of your brain's mechanics can shape your business tactics, influence decisions, and bolster your success as a woman navigating the vibrant business terrain today.

Unlocking Brain Adaptability: Explore neuroplasticity, the brain's remarkable ability to evolve and adjust, and how this can be a game-changer for female business owners. Chat about how fostering a mindset geared toward growth and continuous learning can spark creativity and fortitude in your business pursuits.

Mastering Emotional Smarts: Look into how emotional smarts, or emotional intelligence (EI), play a crucial role in the entrepreneurial world and how women can harness these skills to improve how they communicate, collaborate, and make decisions in the business arena.

Tackling Stress and Bouncing Back: Talk about the brain science behind stress and bouncing back, zeroing in on how to handle stress like a pro and build resilience when the going gets tough. Shed light on how women entrepreneurs can use stress to their advantage, spurring growth while keeping their mental wellness in check during their business adventures.

Sidestepping Mental Traps: Examine the mental traps, or cognitive biases, that can skew business decisions and discuss how women at the helm of businesses can avoid falling for them. Tips for thinking clearly, gaining new perspectives, and making sound, informed decisions in the entrepreneurial world need to be offered in female entrepreneur.

Igniting Creativity and Pioneering Innovation: Dive into the brain's role in creativity and innovation, spotlighting ways to kickstart your creative engine and solve problems innovatively. We'll see how women entrepreneurs can tap into their brain's imaginative power to forge novel concepts and stand out in the competitive business marketplace.

Forming Winning Habits and Routines: Chat about the brain science behind habits and routines, stressing the significance of crafting deliberate habits for productivity and triumph in business. Be guided through setting up beneficial habits, fine-tuning your daily patterns, and keeping your focus and discipline sharp as a businesswoman.

Boosting Confidence and Belief in Your Abilities: Delve into the neural underpinnings of confidence and self-belief, discuss how your mindset and convictions shape your actions and results in the business world. Set tactics for building your confidence, pushing past imposter syndrome, and wielding self-belief to chase ambitious targets with assurance.

Winning at Negotiations and Influence: Explore the brainy side of influence and negotiation, looking at how mental shortcuts and social interplay sway decisions in business dealings.

BECOMING YOUR OWN FUTURE

Welcome to "Women Starting Business: Becoming Your Own Future," where we embark on a journey tailored for aspiring female entrepreneurs eager to forge their own success stories.

This series is a deep dive into the transformative process of taking charge of your future as a woman in business, focusing on the mindset, abilities, and tactics necessary to convert aspirations into realities and craft a flourishing business and life.

Discover the Strength of Visionary Leadership: Explore the influential role of visionary leadership in the entrepreneurial world and how women can picture themselves as triumphant business leaders.

It's crucial to have clear objectives, develop a captivating vision, and lead with intention to encourage and drive others.

Championing Personal Growth: Delve into personal growth and self-exploration as key elements in taking control of your future.

Urge female entrepreneurs to commit to ongoing education, introspection, and self-improvement to tap into their ultimate capabilities and reach their dreams.

Redefining Success: Challenge traditional ideas of success and support needs to be supported in defining it on their terms.

Discussing how to align business objectives with your personal values, passions, and life goals that can lead to a rewarding and significant entrepreneurial path.

Breaking Free from Limiting Beliefs: Tackle the limiting beliefs that might prevent you from reaching your entrepreneurial potential.

Women needs to be enlightened on ways to recognize and conquer self-doubt, impostor syndrome, and other hurdles to success, empowering them to embrace their excellence with confidence.

Fostering Resilience and Flexibility: How resilience and adaptability are key to managing the entrepreneurial roller coaster should be examined. Offer methods for developing resilience, recovering from challenges, and viewing change as an avenue for growth and innovation.

Crafting Your Own Path: Inspire women to generate their own opportunities and carve unique success paths.

Highlight the significance of being proactive, grabbing chances, and adopting an entrepreneurial spirit to transform dreams into actionable steps and real outcomes.

Taking Bold Steps: Encourage women to take bold, decisive action toward their business ambitions.

Talk about the importance of embracing calculated risks, venturing beyond comfort zones, and seeing failure as part of the learning and evolving journey.

Valuing Authenticity and Making an Impact: Stress the importance of being authentic and ethical in business, urging women to remain true to themselves and their principles as they grow their ventures.

Discuss how authenticity builds trust, fosters connections, and has a significant impact on business relationships and communities.

Creating a Solid Support System: Emphasize the need for a supportive network of mentors, colleagues, and allies for the entrepreneurial voyage.

Encourage women to connect with mentors for advice, support, and valuable insights drawn from their business experiences.

Achieving Work-Life Harmony: Address the necessity of balancing work and personal life for enduring entrepreneurial success.

Offer tips for prioritizing wellness, establishing boundaries, and blending personal and professional roles for a satisfying and viable lifestyle.

Championing Diversity and Inclusivity: Advocate for diversity and inclusivity in the business sphere, underlining the benefits that varied perspectives, backgrounds, and experiences bring to fostering innovation and creativity.

Encourage women to promote diversity within their businesses and communities, creating a welcoming and supportive environment for everyone.

Driving Positive Change: Motivate women to leverage their businesses as tools for societal betterment and impactful change.

Women Starting Business 2024

YOUR VALUE PROPOSITION

Unveiling Your Business Superpowers: Empowering female founders to pinpoint their superpowers—the distinct talents, knowledge, and abilities they bring to the table. It's all about recognizing what makes them stand out in the crowd and using those superpowers to captivate their ideal customers.

Tapping into Customer Desires: Putting a spotlight on the power of truly getting your customers. It's key for women in business to dive deep, exploring what makes their customers tick, what they're yearning for, and what bothers them. By getting to the heart of their audience's needs, they can tailor their offerings to hit the mark just right.

Offering a Silver Bullet: Zeroing in on that magic bullet that solves a customer's headache or fulfills a craving. It's crucial for female entrepreneurs to articulate exactly how their product or service swoops in to tackle those specific issues or desires, making their business the go-to solution.

Broadcasting What's Special: Encourage women business leaders to broadcast the special perks and advantages their business offers loud and clear. It's about crafting a message that strikes a chord with their audience and spells out why their product or service is the pick of the litter.

Standing Out from the Crowd: Women needs to urge to shine a light on what's unique about their business. What's the secret sauce that sets them apart? Identifying and flaunting these unique aspects helps your business pop in a sea of sameness.

Staying True to Your Brand: Aligning what you stand for with your business's promise to the world. It's about keeping it real and ensuring that every bit of your message is steeped in the values and mission that define your brand.

Embracing Trial and Error: Champion the idea of test-driving your value proposition. It's about staying nimble, learning from customer feedback, and fine-tuning your approach to nail what resonates best with your audience.

Tracking Your Wins: Measure the splash your value proposition makes. By keeping an eye on customer happiness, how many people are taking the bait, and if the cash register is ringing more often, you can gauge how well your message is landing and tweak it for even better results.

Staying on Your Toes: Business Women need to highlight how to keep their fingers on the pulse of the market. Changes and new trends are always around the corner, and staying adaptable means your value proposition can remain fresh and competitive.

Cementing Trust: Emphasize the power of trust and how your value proposition can be a trust magnet. By being reliable, open, and honest, women entrepreneurs can build a loyal customer base that believes in their business.

Wowing with Service: Women at the helm need to be encouraged to make customer experience their ace card. Delivering top-notch, personalized service and smooth interactions can turn happy customers into raving fans.

Putting Customers First: Stress the importance of a customer-first strategy in shaping your value proposition. By tuning into customer feedback and anticipating their needs, women entrepreneurs can ensure their offerings deliver max satisfaction.

Innovating Like a Boss: Women business owners need to be inspired to keep the spirit of innovation alive in their value proposition. By staying creative and open to evolution, they can stay ahead of the game and seize new opportunities that come their way.

Crafting Irresistible Messages: Women should be guided in creating messages that are like honey for their target audience—clear, simple, and consistent across all channels to draw customers in and keep them engaged.

Educating for Empowerment: Women at the helm need to be encouraged to not just sell but also teach and empower their customers. By outlining the awesome outcomes people can expect and supporting them on their journey, they can deepen customer relationships.

Forging Powerful Partnerships: Women should be encouraged to look for allies and partners that can enhance and amplify their value proposition. Collaborating with others can broaden their reach and open doors to new possibilities.

Keeping It Real: Stress the importance of being your authentic self when communicating your value proposition. Genuine, straightforward interactions can build a foundation of trust that stands the test of time.

Scoping Out the Competition: Female entrepreneurs should be guided to keep a watchful eye on the competition and smartly position their value proposition in the arena. It's about playing up what makes them different and better to capture the spotlight.

Celebrating Every Win: It is all about cheering on every victory that comes from a killer value proposition. By taking a moment to celebrate the big and small wins, women entrepreneurs fuel their drive for even greater achievements.

TRANSFER OF WEALTH

Grasping Wealth Transfer: Break down what wealth transfer means, especially for women kicking off their own businesses. It's about the goodies – assets, resources, financial leg-ups – passed down from one generation to the next.

Opening Doors for Women in Business: For women stepping into the entrepreneurial ring, this wealth transfer can be a game-changer. It's about turning that family treasure chest into a launchpad for their business dreams, aiming to keep the wealth ball rolling for generations.

Tackling the Hurdles: It's not always smooth sailing. Women can hit snags like gender biases, a lack of money smarts, or sticky cultural expectations that can put a wrench in using that wealth to its full potential.

Getting Money-Smart: Knowledge is power, right? So, boosting financial know-how is key for women to handle this wealth like pros. Think workshops, courses, and resources to sharpen those financial skills.

Thinking Big (and Long-Term): We're talking strategies that go the distance, lining up with those big entrepreneurial visions. Investing, safeguarding wealth, planning the estate – all that jazz to make sure the wealth sticks around.

Joining Forces: There's strength in numbers. Linking up with mentors, savvy advisors, and fellow business women can make a world of difference in navigating the wealth waters.

Passing the Torch: It's about lighting the way for the next gen of women, using success to fuel education, entrepreneurship, and financial independence for the young ones and the community.

Leveling the Playing Field: Let's face it, the wealth transfer game can be lopsided. Time to shake up those old-school norms and push for equal chances for women entrepreneurs to get their fair share.

Doing Good with the Dough: How about using that wealth to make a splash in the world? We're talking about social impact, philanthropy, and making investments that do some good.

Family Ties: Family and money can mix like oil and water. So, let's navigate those tricky waters with clear chats, conflict-solving tricks, and family agreements to keep everyone on the same page.

Embracing the Entrepreneurial Spirit: Leaning into traits like resilience and creativity can turn that wealth into a powerhouse for business success.

Mixing It Up: Don't put all your eggs in one basket. Diversifying investments can help women entrepreneurs spread risks and up their game.

Expert Backup: Sometimes, you gotta call in the pros – financial gurus, legal eagles, and planning wizards – to tailor a wealth strategy that fits just right.

Taking the Reins: It's about women stepping up and owning their financial destiny, getting savvy, asking the tough questions, and making sure they're a big part of the money talk.

Tech-Savvy Wealth: Tech's changing the game in managing money. Women entrepreneurs can jump on fintech tools and digital platforms to make smarter, faster money moves.

Opening Doors: Push for everyone to get a fair shot at building wealth, especially those who've been left out of the loop. It's about making sure the financial playing field is wide open for all.

Leaving a Mark: Think beyond the bank balance. Aim to leave a legacy that echoes your values and passions, making a dent in the world that'll outlast the dollars.

Daring to Dive In: Encourage women to take calculated risks and get inventive with their investments. It's about seizing new opportunities that could lead to big payoffs.

Cheering On Financial Wins: Women who've turned their inherited wealth into entrepreneurial triumphs need to be celebrated. They're the trailblazers showing the way for the next wave of women in business.

All for One: Foster a spirit of togetherness, where women entrepreneurs, their kin, and communities all pull together, sharing know-how and networks to lift each other up in the wealth game.

CAREGIVING AND LONGEVITY

Exploring the Terrain: Let's talk about the unique hurdles and chances women encounter when they're juggling the roles of caregiver and entrepreneur. It's becoming more common to see women launching their own businesses while also looking after kids, elderly relatives, or family members with special needs.

Mastering the Work-Life Blend: Dive into ways to weave caregiving duties into the entrepreneurial journey. Learn some savvy tips on managing time, setting limits, and crafting work setups that bend to fit caregiving, all while keeping your eyes on the prize - your business objectives.

Tapping into Support Circles: It's crucial to build a solid network for support. Women entrepreneurs, you're not alone! Lean on family, buddies, and community helpers, and don't forget

55

about fellow caregiver and entrepreneur groups online.

Making Time for You: Remember, taking care of yourself is non-negotiable. When you're spinning the plates of business and caregiving, you need your self-care toolbox - think workouts, a moment of zen, and maybe some professional guidance to dodge burnout and stay on top of your game.

Embracing Flexibility in Business: Women need to be encouraged to think about business models that gel with caregiving. Whether it's a home office, an online gig, or a service that you can schedule around your life, flexibility is your friend.

Pushing for Better Policies: Changes in policies and workplace norms that back women doing the double dance of business and caregiving should be champion. Paid family leave, affordable childcare, and tax breaks for flex-friendly businesses are all on the wish list.

Harnessing Tech: Tech can be a game-changer, making remote work, teaming up online, and health services from afar a reality. Look at tools that can tidy up caregiving and keep your business humming along.

Growing Resilience and Flexing with Change: Women should be empowered to become unshakable and versatile in the face of caregiving surprises and business twists. Strategies to handle stress, bounce back, and keep your long-term vision in sight are key.

Planning Finances Wisely: It's vital to talk about money - planning for your business and caregiving needs is a must. You should point toward smart budgeting, saving, and investing to keep you and your loved ones financially secure.

Applauding Women's Achievements: Give a standing ovation to women who are rocking both the entrepreneurial and caregiving worlds. Their success stories are the inspiration we all need.

Championing Work-Life Harmony: Instead of trying to separate work and caregiving, Find ways to blend them. This approach can lead to a more peaceful coexistence of business and family life.

Standing Up for Equal Responsibility: We've got to push for an even playing field when it comes to caregiving. It's time for a cultural shift where everyone's contributions at work and home are valued and shared more equally.

Creating Supportive Workplaces: We should nudge employers and leaders to make workspaces that understand caregiving needs. Flexible hours, remote work options, and maybe even childcare at the office can make a world of difference.

Nurturing Entrepreneurial Spirits: Let's cultivate communities that offer resources and mentorship for women balancing business with caregiving. Connecting with others who get it can be a huge help.

Investing in Yourself: Women, it's time to boost your personal and professional skills. Whether it's through ongoing learning or networking, these opportunities can strengthen your dual role as caregiver and entrepreneur.

Prioritizing Overall Wellness: We're talking about a full-circle approach to health for women juggling business and caregiving. Stress less, care more for yourself, and find that sweet spot of balance.

Advancing Research and Change-Making: We need to push for studies and policies that focus on women's dual roles. More data and advocacy can lead to better decisions and stronger support for women in both arenas.

Forging Strategic Alliances: Women should partner up with groups that get the caregiver-entrepreneur struggle. Working together will help tackle the big obstacles and build a more supportive environment.

Inspiring the Next Wave: The next generation of women need to be empowered to chase their entrepreneurial dreams without sidelining the value of caregiving. Mentoring and education can light the way for young women to make their mark in business and at home.

Celebrating Our Unique Stories: Here's to the rich tapestry of women's experiences in caregiving and entrepreneurship. Inclusivity and representation matter, and they help support women from all walks of life as they navigate these dual paths.

These insights are all about helping women entrepreneurs find their stride at the crossroads of caregiving and business. By embracing the challenges and opportunities that come with caregiving, women can craft successful strategies to flourish in business while caring for their loved ones with heart and determination.

HOW TO BE PAID WHAT YOU ARE WORTH

Understanding Your Worth: It's crucial for female entrepreneurs to grasp their true value. Dive into market research, evaluate your skills and experience, and compare your prices with industry norms to ensure you're on the right track.

Crafting Smart Pricing Plans: It's key to develop sharp, competitive pricing strategies for your offerings. Delve into various pricing methods like cost-plus, value-based, and competitive pricing to find the sweet spot for profit and value perception.

Expressing Your Unique Offer: Make sure to communicate the special benefits and value your business brings to the table. Show potential clients why you're the go-to expert in your field.

Bargaining with Boldness: Step into negotiations with assurance and poise. Arm yourself with negotiation know-how to champion your worth and the quality of your work.

Designing Attractive Packages: Consider offering bundles or packages to boost value perception and ask for better prices. Tailor different pricing levels to meet the needs and wants of various customer groups.

Showcasing Success and Value: It's important to show the tangible results and ROI your business provides. Gather glowing testimonials and solid case studies to back up your pricing.

Building a Standout Brand: A strong brand pulls in premium prices and top-tier clients. Focus on creating a memorable brand identity, nurturing customer relationships, and delivering top-notch service to stand out.

Providing Payment Flexibility: Offering varied payment options can cater to a range of customer needs while ensuring you're compensated fairly.

Tapping into Your Network: Use your professional circles to find new opportunities and higher-paying gigs. Networking can be a goldmine for expanding your business and boosting your income.

Committing to Growth and Learning: Keep sharpening your skills and knowledge to command higher pay. Look for training and mentorship that will give you an edge in the market.

Reviewing Prices Regularly: Make it a habit to reassess and tweak your prices based on market shifts and your business performance.

Getting Expert Input: Don't shy away from consulting financial pros or business mentors to craft pricing strategies that work for you.

Staying Industry-Savvy: Keep an eye on the pulse of your industry, including pricing trends and benchmarks, to stay competitive.

Offering Top-Shelf Services: Consider providing specialized or luxury services for niche or high-end markets to justify premium rates.

Embracing Self-Belief: Hold onto confidence and a sense of abundance when setting your prices. Remember, you're worth it!

Maximizing Specialized Skills: Leverage your unique skills and knowledge to demand higher prices that reflect your specialized expertise.

Clarifying Pricing Upfront: Be transparent with your pricing to build trust and avoid confusion with clients.

Adding Extra Value: Think about including additional services that elevate the customer experience and support higher pricing.

Cultivating Lasting Connections: Long-term client relationships can lead to repeat business and referrals, all thanks to trust and consistent value delivery.

Knowing Your Boundaries: Recognize when to walk away from deals that don't meet your value or pricing standards.

Adjusting Prices with Agility: Stay flexible and ready to modify your pricing in response to feedback and business objectives.

Gathering Glowing Reviews: Positive feedback can validate your prices and strengthen your value proposition.

Focusing on Quality: Prioritize delivering superb quality that warrants premium pricing and ensures long-term success.

Positioning as a Premium Choice: Aim to position your business as a high-end brand that attracts discerning clients willing to pay more.

Defending Your Pricing: Be ready to explain your pricing choices and highlight the value you offer to any doubters.

Pursuing Perpetual Progress: Stay open to enhancing your pricing approach based on customer feedback and market evolution.

Standing Out with Stellar Service: Personalized service can set you apart and justify higher prices.

Investing in Marketing: Put resources into marketing and branding to convey your value and draw in the right clients.

Aligning Prices with Ambitions: Ensure your pricing reflects your business aspirations and the value you deliver to clients.

Staying Faithful to Your Value: Stand firm on your worth, even when it's tough. Maintain excellence, and the right compensation will follow.

WRITING YOUR BUSINESS PLAN

Introduction to Crafting Your Business Blueprint: Stress the critical role of a business blueprint in guiding entrepreneurs toward success. It's not just paperwork for investors; it's a strategic compass for the entrepreneur to define their vision, establish objectives, and steer their decision-making.

Executive Overview: Touch on the essentials of the executive overview, which gives a snapshot of your business blueprint. Urge female entrepreneurs to concisely present their business idea, target audience, distinctive edge, and financial summaries to pique interest and showcase the venture's promise.

Business Narrative: Advise female entrepreneurs on how to elaborate on their business idea, including their offerings, intended audience, market analysis, and competitive scene. Urge them to express their purpose, aspirations, and principles, as well as any standout features or competitive edges that set their business apart.

Market Examination: Talk about the significance of a deep dive into the market to grasp industry movements, consumer desires, and the competitive field. Urge female entrepreneurs to investigate market patterns, customer profiles, and competitor tactics to pinpoint opportunities and shape their business strategy.

Marketing and Sales Approach: Assist female entrepreneurs in formulating an all-encompassing marketing and sales plan to draw customers and drive income. Discuss aspects like branding, pricing, distribution paths, and promotional methods designed to effectively engage the target audience and boost sales.

Operations and Leadership Blueprint: Describe the business's operational and leadership framework, including an organizational diagram, key team members, and operational workflows.

Urge female entrepreneurs to detail daily operations, production or service execution, quality control, and leadership duties to ensure seamless business functioning.

Financial Forecasts: Offer advice on projecting financials, including profit and loss statements, cash flow estimates, and balance sheets. Urge female entrepreneurs to forecast income, expenses, and profitability over a set duration, taking into account factors that impact financial outcomes.

Funding Needs: Discuss capital requirements and financial avenues to back the startup and expansion of the business. Guide female entrepreneurs in evaluating their funding needs, exploring sources like savings, loans, grants, or investors, and explaining how the funds will be deployed to reach business aims.

Risk Strategy and Backup Plans: Accentuate the need for identifying and curtailing risks with proactive risk strategy and backup plans. Urge female entrepreneurs to evaluate potential hazards and challenges, devise mitigation tactics, and plan for unexpected events or disruptions.

Rollout Timeline: Aid female entrepreneurs in developing a practical rollout timeline that details crucial milestones, tasks, and deadlines for launching and expanding the business. Urge them to prioritize tasks, allocate resources wisely, and monitor progress to ensure the business blueprint's timely execution.

Performance Monitoring: Highlight the necessity of regular performance reviews to track advancement, assess outcomes, and tweak strategies when needed. Urge female entrepreneurs to set key metrics, establish success benchmarks, and periodically refine their business blueprint based on feedback and insights.

Legal and Regulatory Adherence: Talk about the legal and regulatory obligations related to the business, such as licenses, permits, contracts, and intellectual property rights. Guide female entrepreneurs in complying with relevant laws to sidestep legal issues and safeguard their business interests.

Ethical Business Practices: Emphasize the importance of ethical behavior and responsible business methods. Urge female entrepreneurs to prioritize honesty, openness, and societal responsibility in their operations, choices, and stakeholder interactions.

Professional Presentation: Stress the importance of a professionally presented business blueprint. Provide tips on formatting, structure, and language to ensure clarity and readability. Urge female entrepreneurs to seek critiques and make revisions to polish their blueprint before presenting it to stakeholders.

Ongoing Refinement: Emphasize that business planning is a recurring process that benefits from regular refinement and adaptation. Urge female entrepreneurs to welcome feedback, learn from experiences, and continually update their business blueprint to reflect market shifts, customer input, and evolving business objectives.

Mentorship and Support: Urge female entrepreneurs to seek wisdom and support from seasoned business owners and industry experts.

Discuss the benefits of networking, mentorship programs, and peer support groups for gaining insights, tackling hurdles, and building confidence.

Acknowledging Achievements: Celebrate the progress and milestones of female entrepreneurs on their business journey. Highlight the value of recognizing victories, honoring achievements, and commemorating milestones to stay driven and inspired.

Cultivating a Growth Attitude: Urge female entrepreneurs to embrace a mindset of resilience, flexibility, and eagerness to learn and expand. Discuss the benefits of facing challenges head-on, learning from setbacks, and seizing chances to innovate and grow as business leaders.

Women's Business Empowerment: Empower female entrepreneurs to take the reins of their business planning and carve their path to triumph. Discuss the power of self-assurance and determination in conquering obstacles and fulfilling entrepreneurial aspirations.

Economic Contribution: Shine a light on the broader impact of women-led businesses in fostering economic empowerment, innovation, and societal progress. Discuss how women's entrepreneurship contributes to job creation, economic expansion, and community advancement.

Networking and Teamwork: Urge female entrepreneurs to tap into networking and forge partnerships with fellow business owners, industry professionals, and potential allies. Discuss the advantages of networking events, industry gatherings, and online forums for making connections, exchanging knowledge, and finding collaborative opportunities that can propel business growth.

Staying Current with Market Trends: Highlight the need to keep up with market trends, customer preferences, and industry updates to inform business planning and strategy. Urge female entrepreneurs to stay in tune with market forces, conduct market research, and adjust their business plans to leverage new opportunities and minimize risks.

Building Resilience and Nimbleness: Discuss the importance of resilience and nimbleness in tackling the uncertainties and challenges of entrepreneurship. Urge female entrepreneurs to build resilience by accepting setbacks, learning from failures, and adapting to changes with agility and creativity.

Investing in Personal Growth: Urge female entrepreneurs to prioritize self-improvement and continuous learning to bolster their skills, knowledge, and capabilities as business leaders. Discuss the benefits of investing in education, training, and skill enhancement to empower women to excel in their ventures and overcome challenges.

Feedback and Validation: Stress the value of seeking input and validation from mentors, advisors, and target customers throughout the business planning process. Urge female entrepreneurs to welcome constructive criticism, test assumptions, and confirm business concepts to align with market demands and preferences.

Financial Vigilance and Adaptability: Highlight the importance of keeping an eye on financial health and key metrics to guide decision-making and track progress. Urge female entrepreneurs to review financial reports, analyze variances, and modify strategies as necessary to meet financial objectives and sustain business momentum.

Innovative and Creative Spirit: Encourage a culture of innovation and creativity in women-owned businesses by promoting experimentation, risk-taking, and out-of-the-box thinking. Discuss how innovation fosters competitiveness, distinction, and long-term success in today's ever-changing business landscape.

Diversity and Inclusion Advocacy: Champion diversity and inclusion in entrepreneurship by creating welcoming spaces for women from various backgrounds, viewpoints, and experiences. Discuss the positive impact of diversity on innovation, teamwork, and catering to a diverse customer base.

Work-Life Harmony: Support female entrepreneurs in managing work-life balance by advocating strategies for maintaining equilibrium, prioritizing effectively, and caring for oneself.

Discuss the importance of setting boundaries, delegating responsibilities, and self-care to preserve well-being and long-term business and personal success.

Honoring Women Entrepreneurs: Celebrate the impact and successes of women entrepreneurs in spurring economic growth, innovation, and societal transformation. Spotlight inspiring stories, role models, and pioneers who motivate and empower women to chase their entrepreneurial dreams and make a lasting difference in their communities and beyond.

BECOMING AUTHENTIC

Starting a Business as a Woman. Embracing the Real You is Important

Diving into Authenticity: Let's talk about authenticity—it's about your actions, values, beliefs, and identity all being in sync. For entrepreneurs, being authentic is key because it builds trust and credibility with everyone you do business with.

Discovering What You Stand For: As a female entrepreneur, it's crucial to figure out your core values and beliefs. These are the things that define you and guide your leadership and business decisions. Take some time to reflect and get clear on what matters most to you.

Matching Personal Values with Your Business: It's super important to make sure your personal values vibe with your business's mission.

When you start a business, make sure it reflects what you're passionate about. This mission will be your north star, guiding you through your business journey.

Learning to Be Real and Imperfect: Let go of trying to be perfect. Being real and showing your vulnerabilities can actually help you connect with people and make your business relationships more genuine.

Creating True Connections: Aim to build real, honest relationships with customers, team members, and partners. Being empathetic, open, and true to yourself can help create lasting bonds that are great for business.

Being Yourself in Branding and Marketing: When it comes to branding and marketing, let your true self shine. Use language and stories that are real and that speak to your audience, making sure they capture the essence of your brand.

Leading with Your True Self: Authentic leadership is about being honest, ethical, and humble. Lead by example and inspire your team to create a culture of trust and teamwork.

Celebrating Your Unique Self: Your individuality and diverse experiences are your superpowers in business. Embrace what makes you different—authenticity is about being yourself, not fitting into a mold.

Staying Self-Aware and Reflective: Keep checking in with yourself to make sure you're staying true to your values and goals. Being self-aware and reflective is key to staying authentic in both life and business.

Resisting Pressure to Conform: Stay strong against outside pressures and expectations that might try to sway you from being yourself. Trust your gut and follow your own path, even if others might not get it.

Making Customer Experiences Personal: Create customer experiences that are true to your values and brand. Listen to your customers, value their input, and provide interactions that are personal and build trust.

Encouraging Authenticity at Work: Work on making your company culture one where everyone can be themselves. Encourage open communication and celebrate everyone's unique contributions.

Being Transparent and Accountable: Make sure you're open and accountable in how you run your business. Owning up to mistakes and being transparent can really boost trust with everyone involved in your business.

Communicating with Heart: When you talk to people, be it your team or customers, do it with sincerity and care. Authentic communication is all about being genuine and listening well.

Sticking to Your Vision: Keep your eyes on your vision and purpose, especially when things get tough. Being committed to your values and goals is crucial for making it through the ups and downs of running a business.

Learning from Mistakes: Don't be afraid of failure—it's all part of the journey. Use it to learn and grow, and take feedback as a chance to become even more authentic in how you do business.

Finding Role Models Who Get It: Look for mentors who are all about being real and leading with purpose. They can show you the ropes and inspire you to be an authentic leader.

Dealing with Gender Bias: Gender bias is real, but don't let it shake you. Stay true to who you are, push against stereotypes, and use your authenticity as your strength, especially in industries where women are underrepresented.

Balancing Professionalism with Being Real: It's possible to be both professional and authentic. Find that sweet spot where you can be taken seriously while still being your genuine self.

Inspiring Authenticity in Others: Encourage others to find their authentic leadership style. Create chances for mentorship and growth in your business, and help shape future leaders who value integrity and purpose.

By sticking to your authentic self, you'll forge deeper connections and make a lasting impact with your business. This guide is all about helping you, as a woman starting a business, to harness the power of authenticity every step of the way.

PHILANTHROPY

Starting a Business with a Heart for Giving

Let's chat about philanthropy – it's all about sharing your blessings, whether that's money, time, or a helping hand, to make our world a better place. It's super important because it's not just about giving; it's about making a real difference.

When women start businesses, they've got this amazing chance to weave their love for helping others right into their company's DNA. Imagine running a business that not only makes money but also makes the world shine a little brighter. That's what values-driven entrepreneurship is all about.

It's cool to build a business where everyone's all about giving back. It boosts the team spirit, makes work more meaningful, and connects us with our neighbors. Plus, it's good for business – happy employees and a happy community can lead to a thriving company.

For women at the helm of their own ships, it's all about finding those causes that make your heart beat faster and matching them with your business goals. Dig deep, chat with folks, and figure out where you can really make a splash with your generosity.

And hey, why go it alone? Teaming up with charities and community groups can make your efforts go further. It's like joining forces with superheroes – together, you can tackle bigger challenges and make a bigger impact.

Let's not forget about the power of our teams. When employees roll up their sleeves and get involved, magic happens. It's not just about donating cash; it's about sharing what we're good at and where we can help out.

Speaking of money, it's a big deal. When women entrepreneurs set aside some of their hard-earned profits for a good cause, they're directly fueling change and supporting those in need.

And let's get creative with how we spread the word. Cause marketing isn't just about selling; it's about starting conversations and getting people to rally around important issues.

But how do we know we're making a dent? It's all about tracking our impact and sharing the wins. It shows we're serious about making a difference and holds us accountable to our promises.

Now, let's think big – global big. Our businesses can be a force for good all over the planet, tackling worldwide issues and joining hands across borders.

A big part of giving back is lifting up women and girls. By focusing on education and empowerment, we're not just helping individuals; we're investing in brighter futures for everyone.

Let's not forget our planet. It's our home, and businesses can play a huge role in keeping it healthy. Whether it's going green or supporting environmental causes, every little bit helps.

Getting involved in the community isn't just nice; it's necessary. It's about standing up for what's right and using our business as a platform for change.

And let's inspire the next bunch of leaders to carry the torch of giving. When we set an example, we're showing them how it's done and encouraging a cycle of generosity.

Diversity and inclusion should be at the heart of our giving. It's about making sure everyone gets a fair shot and that we're listening to all voices.

Finally, let's give a big shout-out to the women entrepreneurs who are already crushing it in the giving game. Their stories and successes light the way for the rest of us to follow.

So, for all you women out there starting your own thing, remember: your business can be a powerhouse of change. Let's make our mark, not just in the business world, but in making the world a kinder, better place for everyone.

RETIREMENT

Starting Your Own Business? Don't Forget Retirement Planning!

Let's talk about why it's crucial for you, as a woman entrepreneur, to think about retirement from the get-go. You've got unique hurdles and chances when it comes to saving for your golden years, like living longer, dealing with income hiccups, and making sure you're set when work becomes a choice, not a necessity.

First things first, take a good look at your money situation. Know what's coming in, what's going out, and where you stand with savings and debts. It's like setting the stage for your retirement plan.

Now, dream a little – what does your perfect retirement look like? Get clear on your goals, whether it's sipping margaritas on the beach at 60 or launching a new venture at 70. Remember to factor in the rising cost of living and those pesky health bills.

Let's dive into the retirement account pool – IRAs, 401(k)s, SEP-IRAs, you name it. Each one comes with its perks and tax quirks, so let's find the perfect fit for you.

Max out those contributions whenever you can. It's like planting seeds now for a lush retirement garden later. Plus, the tax benefits? Chef's kiss!

Investment portfolios can be a bit like a complex recipe, but don't worry – I'll help you mix the right ingredients for growth and income when you retire. A pinch of asset allocation, a dash of diversification, and voilà!

Healthcare costs in retirement are no joke, so let's make sure you're covered. Medicare, private insurance – we'll sort through it and set aside some dough for those unexpected health hiccups.

Ever thought about making money while you sleep? Let's chat about creating multiple income streams for retirement – real estate, stocks, even that side hustle could keep the cash flowing.

Living a long, healthy life is great, but it also means your money has to last. We'll explore ways to stretch your savings, like annuities or holding off on Social Security to get the most bang for your buck.

Speaking of Social Security, there's a strategy to it. We'll figure out when and how to claim your benefits to maximize your retirement paycheck.

Estate planning isn't just for the rich and famous. Let's make sure your hard-earned wealth goes exactly where you want it to when the time comes – your kids, charity, or that little bookshop you've always wanted to open.

Retirement might mean tweaking your lifestyle, but it's not all about cutting corners. It's finding that sweet spot between enjoying life and keeping your bank account happy.

Sure, you're a savvy businesswoman, but even pros need advice. A financial planner can be your retirement BFF, offering personalized tips to steer you right.

Life loves throwing curveballs, especially when it comes to money. So, keep your retirement plan as flexible as your yoga instructor, ready to bend and stretch as needed.

Knowledge is power, especially with money. Let's boost your financial smarts so you can make choices that feel right for you, not just now but all the way to retirement.

If you're thinking about slowing down or switching gears work-wise, let's chat about how that fits into your retirement vision. Maybe it's consulting, part-time work, or finally writing that novel.

Work-life balance isn't just a buzzword; it's key for a happy retirement. We'll talk about how to juggle business, fun, and family time so you can savor every moment.

And when you hit those retirement milestones, take a moment to pat yourself on the back. You've earned it! Financial independence and security are worth celebrating – they mean freedom, peace of mind, and the chance to live retirement on your terms.

So, as you build your empire, keep one eye on the retirement prize. With a little planning and some savvy moves, you'll be all set for a future that's as bright and bold as you are. Let's make it happen!

Women Starting Business 2024

www.ingramcontent.com/pod-product-compliance
Lightning Source LLC
Chambersburg PA
CBHW070311230526
45470CB00002B/829